St. Mary's High School

# A FRUITFUL BRANCH
## ON THE VINE,
### JESUS

First book
of Mother Teresa of Calcutta
edited
by Missionaries of Charity

# Mother Teresa of Calcutta

# A FRUITFUL BRANCH
# ON THE VINE,
# JESUS

**ST. ANTHONY MESSENGER PRESS**

Cincinnati, Ohio

*Nihil Obstat*
Romae, E Pontificia Universitate Lateranense
die 9 Septembris 1998
+Angelus Scola, Rector

*Imprimatur*
E Vicariatu Urbis
die 14 Septembris 1998
+Aloysius Moretti, Segretarius Generalis

*Art Director:* Giacomo Callo
*Graphic Designer:* Francesca Leoneschi
*Cover image:* Mother Teresa of Calcutta

Originally published in Italian under the title *Ti offro il mio cuore, o Signore*, by Arnoldo Mondadori Editore S.p.A., Milan, Italy, copyright © 1998 Arnoldo Mondadori Editore S.p.A., Milano

Published in English by St. Anthony Messenger Press
by special arrangement with Arnoldo Mondadori Editore.

ISBN 0-86716-424-7
English edition copyright © 2000, St. Anthony Messenger Press
Printed in the U.S.A.
www.AmericanCatholic.org

# Index

*Archbishop Henry D'Souza*
Archbishop of Calcutta

**ARCHBISHOP'S HOUSE**
32, PARK STREET
CALCUTTA-700 016

Telephone : 2471980
FAX. 00-91-33-2474666

7.7.98

Sr Nirmala,
Superior General,
Missionaries of Charity,
Calcutta

Dear Sr. Nirmala,

As the first death anniversay of Mother Teresa approaches, I would like to dedicate these few lines to her,.

Mother Teresa was world famous in her life time, and since her death she has become a legend. Hundreds of people visit her tomb, and ask for favours. Many go away with deep peace and joy in their hearts.

May this first anniversary of her death be a moment of recommitment to her spirit. May she help us find the Lord in His many distressing disguises of the poor.

With blessings for yourself and your communites,

I remain,

Yours sincerely in Our Lord,

H. D'Souza
Archbishop of Calcutta

**MISSIONARIES OF CHARITY**

This booklet entitled Mother Teresa, M.C., a Faithful Living Branch on the Vine, Jesus, has been prepared by the "Missionaries of Charity" for the celebration, in Rome, of Mother Teresa's first death anniversary. We hope that it will lead all who choose to read it to a clearer understanding of, and a deeper participation in the Charism (special grace) that Mother Teresa received from God for the good of the Church. It is this Charism that animates the beautiful works of God's love and compassion among the poorest of the poor carried out throughout the world through the faithful, loving cooperation of our dearest Mother who considered herself just a "pencil in God's hands". We ask all who read this book to pray for us that, in carrying on the work entrusted to our Mother, we do not spoil God's Work of Love.

God bless you

*M. Niswala M.c*

Superior General

Calcutta, 22nd august 1998

**A note regarding the text**

The simple drawings of the first section, prepared by the Missionaries of Charity (better known as Sisters of Mother Teresa of Calcutta), are eloquent signs meant to help the reader to understand, without using many words, the spirit that animates Mother Teresa's work.

Why has a section on prayer been added? Because prayer has been the soul and strength of Mother Teresa. These simple prayers have animated her day lived for God, at the service of the poorest of the poor, and they continue to animate the hours of the day of the Missionaries of Charity, because

"the fruit of Prayer is Love, and the fruit of Love is Service".

*(Mother Teresa)*

## Mother Teresa of Calcutta
# A Fruitful Branch on the Vine, JESUS

*Jesus is our prayer
and He is also the answer
to all our prayer*

I THIRST

# "God thirsts to be thirsted for"

*Deus sitit sitire*
(St Augustine)

"I Thirst" Jesus said on the Cross, when He was deprived of every consolation, dying in absolute poverty, left alone, despised, broken in body and soul. He spoke of His Infinite Thirst for love – for souls.

EXPLANATION TO THE ORIGINAL CONSTITUTIONS

# A call within a call

*The root of Mother Teresa's vocation was the experience of Jesus'*
*Thirst for her love in the train ride to Darjeeling on*

### 10th september 1946
*INSPIRATION DAY*

I knew it was His will and I had to follow him to those
who, like Jesus, had nowhere to lay their head... the
naked, despised, forsaken, forgotten, broken... there was
no doubt it was to be His work... the message was quite
clear... it was an order... I knew where I belonged, but I did
not know how to get there, how it would be accompli-
shed, but so let myself be used by God in His way, un-
known to me.

FROM MOTHER'S EARLY WRITINGS

I SATIATE

# *The response*

*The strength it took to face the streets of Calcutta alone was an indication of her conviction.*

*Mother writes:*

God wants me to be a free nun covered with the poverty of the cross... The poverty of the poor must be often so hard for them. The life of Loreto came to tempt me... but of my own free choice... my God, out of love for You I desire to remain and do whatever is Your will in my regard. Give me the courage now, this moment to persevere in following Your care.

*For our Mother, her whole aim, the sole purpose of her leaving the convent of Loreto was in order to quench His Thirst where He thirsted most, among the poorest of the poor.*

# The aim

*In answering God's call Mother Teresa prepared the path for those of us who would have the same call to quench the Thirst of Jesus.*

*In Mother's early writings we read:*

Jesus is God, therefore His Love, His Thirst is infinite. Our aim is to quench the infinite Thirst of a God made man. Just like the adoring angels in heaven ceaselessly sing the praise of God, so the sisters, using the four vows of absolute poverty, chastity, obedience and charity towards the poor ceaselessly quench the Thirsting God by their love and the love of the souls they bring to Him... by living the life of perfect charity in the practice of their four vows the sisters quench Jesus' Thirst for love.

EXPLANATION TO THE ORIGINAL CONSTITUTIONS

I THIRST

# *The motive*

*Mother was drawn to the cross as Jesus himself was, for the salvation of souls.*

*Mother writes:*

Christ's love led Him to Gethsemane and to Calvary. Sin did it... ours and the sins of the world...
Christ hangs before us on the cross crying out

"I Thirst"

It's to quench the Thirst of this divine God that the Missionaries of Charity do all that seems madness to the world. We are blessed, truly blessed in having a little share in the following of the cross.

Love to be true has to hurt.

# The Bread of Life
## Mother's strength

*It was through contact with the Eucharistic Christ that Mother received her outstanding graces and the strength to follow her convictions. This is so clearly seen in the life of our Mother and her teachings.*

*Mother teaches that:*

In each of our lives Jesus comes as

"Bread of Life"

to be eaten as the hungry, thirsty one. Jesus is left alone in the tabernacle, we must love him more, keep ourselves free for Jesus alone. Tell him often "I love you" by caring for all the unwanted, unloved, lonely... all the poor. This is how I quench the Thirst of Jesus for others, by giving Him *love in action*. By each little action done for the sick and the dying I quench the Thirst of Jesus for love.

If you really love Jesus in the Eucharist, you will naturally want to put that love into action. We cannot separate these... the Eucharist and the poor.

*As Missionaries of Charity we are called to see Christ in the Eucharist and to touch Him in the distressing disguise of the poorest of the poor.*

# *The divine living contact*

*Mother says:*

We quench the Thirst of Jesus by
adoration of Jesus
in the Blessed Sacrament,
that personal meeting Him face to face.
Renew your zeal to quench His Thirst under
the appearance of bread
and in
the distressing disguise of the
poorest of the poor."

*"You did it to me."*

Never seperate these words of Jesus

*"I thirst"*

and

*"You did it to me".*

## IMMACULATE HEART OF MARY,
## CAUSE OF OUR JOY, PRAY FOR US

*The emblem of our Congregation consists of a map of the world in an oval shape with India at the center, encircled by a Rosary with the rays from the Cross spreading from Calcutta throughout the world.*

# *In the heart of Mary*
# *Cause of our joy*

*Mother writes in the Constitutions:*

Our Society was born at our Lady's pleading and through her intercession it grew up.

CONSTITUTION 7

*Mother teaches us:*

Love for Mary, we can learn only on our knees and through our Rosary... Let us, my children, give our Lady full liberty to use us for the glory of Her Son, for if we really belong to her, then our holiness is secure. Let us improve our praying the Rosary when we are out of the house. Let us ask our Lady in our own simple way to teach us how to pray – as she taught Jesus – in all the years He was with her in Nazareth... Try to bring our Lady fully into your life, in the community and in the houses of the poor.

# *The spirit of our Society*

*Mother writes:*

> The spirit of our Society is one of
> loving trust
> total surrender
> cheerfulness

*Mother teaches us:*

Today more than ever, we need to pray
for the light to do the will of God,
for the love to accept the will of God,
for the way to do the will of God.

Jesus came to do the Will of the Father, and did it unto death, death on the Cross... the surest way to true holiness and the fulfilment of our mission of peace, love and joy is through obedience.

# *Cheerfulness*

*Mother teaches that:*

Joy is prayer, joy is strength,
joy is love,
a net of love by which to catch souls.

God loves a cheerful giver;
he gives most who gives with joy.

The best way to show your gratitude
to God and people is to
accept everything with joy.

A sister filled with joy is like
the sunshine of God's love,
the hope of eternal happiness,
the flame of burning love.

Never let anything so fill you with
sorrow as to make you forget
the joy of the risen Christ.

*Poverty is love
before it is
renunciation.*

MOTHER TERESA

# *Poverty is our dowry*

Our Lord gives us a living example:

> "Foxes have holes and birds
> of the air their nests, but
> the Son of Man has nowhere
> to lay his head".

From the very first day of His existence Jesus was brought up in a poverty which no human being will ever be able to experience, because...

> "being rich He made Himself poor".

As I am his co-worker, I must be brought up and nourished by that poverty which our Lord asks of me.

We do not accept poverty because we are forced to be poor, but because we choose to be poor for the love of Jesus.

I THIRST

LOVE IN ACTION

# The mission

The greatness of our vocation lies in the fact that we are called to minister to Christ himself in the distressing disguise of the poor and suffering. We are called upon every day, like the priest at Mass, to handle the body of Christ in the form of a suffering humanity, and to give Jesus to all whom we come in contact with, by spreading

> the fragrance of His love
> wherever we go.

Let each one of us see Jesus Christ in the person of the poor. The more repugnant the work or the persons, the greater must be our faith, love and cheerful devotion, ministering to our Lord in his distressing disguise.

*I will give saints and martyrs to Mother Church*

Time is coming closer, when Mother also has to go to God. Then Mother will be able to help each one of you more, guide you more and obtain more graces for you.

WORDS SPOKEN BY MOTHER
TO HER SISTERS ON OCT. 1, 1977

# *For the glory of God*

*On 5th september, 1997, our dearest Mother was called back home to Jesus to hear the welcoming words:*

Come ye blessed of my Father, inherit the Kingdom pre-
pared for you from the foundation of the world, for...
I was hungry and you gave me food,
I was thirsty and you gave me drink,
I was a stranger and you welcomed me,
I was naked and you clothed me,
I was sick and you visited me,
I was in prison, you came to see me.
... truly, truly I say unto you
as often as you did it to one of my least brothers
                    YOU DID IT TO ME.

MATT. 25: 34-36, 40

The fruit of SILENCE is Prayer
The fruit of PRAYER is Faith
The fruit of FAITH is Love
The fruit of LOVE is Service
The fruit of SERVICE is Peace

*God bless you*
*M Teresa MC*

Mary, Mother of Jesus,
be a Mother to me now.

# Mother Teaching Us To Pray

"How do we learn to pray?"
"By praying."

" 6. Jesus, only love of my heart I wish to suffer what I suffer and all Thou wilt have me suffer, for Thy pure love, not because of the merits I may acquire, nor for the rewards Thou hast promised me but only to please thee, to praise thee, to bless thee as well in sorrow as in joy "

August 1948

Missionaries of Charity

"O Jesus, only love of my heart I wish to suffer what I suffer and all that Thou wilt have me suffer, for Thy pure love, not because of the merits I may acquire, nor for the rewards Thou hast promised me but only to please Thee, to praise Thee, to bless Thee as well in sorrow as in joy."

†

*August 1948*                    Missionaries of Charity

Immaculate Heart of Mary
Cause of our joy bless
your own Missionaries
of Charity, help us to do
all the good we can. Keep us
in your most Pure Heart
so that we may please
Jesus and so bring many
Souls to Jesus.
    Let us pray
        God bless you
        M Teresa mc

MH. 1996 Dec.

Immaculate Heart of Mary
Cause of our joy bless
your own Missionaries
of Charity, help us to do
all the good we can, keep us
in your most Pure Heart
so that we may please
Jesus and so bring many
souls to Jesus.

Let us pray

God bless you
M. Teresa M.C.

M.H. 1996 DEC.

Immaculate Heart
of Mary, Cause of our
Joy, bless your own
Missionaries of Charity
help us to do all the
good we can, keep us
in your most pure
Heart, so that we
may please Jesus
through You, in
Him and with you
Amen.

Make Our Lady your
Mother. She will help
to be a holy Sister

Rome / 16-7-97

Immaculate Heart
of Mary, Cause of our
Joy, bless your own
Missionaries of Charity
help us to do all the
good we can, keep us
in your most pure
Heart, so that we
may please Jesus
through You, in
You and with You.
Make Our Lady your
Mother. She will help
to be a holy Sister.

*Rome, 16-7-97*

Mary my dearest Mother,
    give me your heart
so beautiful, so pure, so
immaculate, so full of Love
and Humility, that I may
receive Jesus as you did.
and go in haste to give Him
        to others.
            God bless you
                M Teresa Mc
                    10/9/75

Mary, my dearest Mother,
    give me your heart
so beautiful, so pure, so
immaculate, so full of Love
and Humility, that I may
receive Jesus as You did –
and go in haste to give Him
            to others.

God bless you

M. Teresa M.C.

*10-9-75*

To me, Jesus is
the Word - to be spoken,
the Bread of Life - to be eaten,
the Hungry - to be fed,
and the Thirsty - to be satiated.

To me, Jesus is
the Word – to be spoken,
the Bread of Life – to be eaten,
the Hungry – to be fed,
and the Thirsty – to be satiated.

Mary, Mother of Jesus, and my Mother,
you were the first one to hear Jesus cry,
"I Thirst". You know how real, how deep
is His longing for me and for the poor.
I am yours.

Mother Mary, teach me, bring me
face to face with the Love in the
Heart of Jesus Crucified. With your
help, I will listen to Jesus' Thirst and
it will be for me a Word of Life.

Standing near you, I will give Him
my love, and I will give Him the
chance to love me, and so be the
Cause of Your Joy and so to satiate
Jesus' Thirst for Love of souls. Amen.

M. Teresa mc
June 1997

Mary, Mother of Jesus, and my Mother,
you were the first one to hear Jesus cry,
"I Thirst". You know how real, how deep
is His longing for me and for the poor.
I am yours.

Mother Mary, teach me, bring me
face to face with the Love in the
Heart of Jesus Crucified. With your
help, I will listen to Jesus' Thirst and
it will be for me a Word of Life.

Standing near you, I will give Him
my love, and I will give Him the
chance to love me, and so be the
Cause of Your Joy and so to satiate
Jesus' Thirst for Love of souls. Amen.

M. Teresa M.C.
*June 1997*

May Gods blessing be with you
Always pray together
and
You will stay together
and
love each other as
Jesus loves each one
of You
God bless you
M Teresa m.c.

May Gods blessing be with you
Always pray together
and
You will stay together
and
love each other as
Jesus loves each one for you

God bless you
M. Teresa M.C.

J.D.M.                    New York, 21- 6- 97

My dearest children.
            Holy Innocents
May God's blessing be
with you all - and
help you to grow
in prayer. for better
is your prayer the closer
you come to Jesus and
Mary and the closer you get
the more you grow in that love
for Jesus and Mary
    Let us pray
                God bless you
                    M. Teresa mc

52

L.D.M.*                    New York, 21-6-97

My dearest children,
            Holy Innocents
May Gods blessing be
with you all – and
help you to grow
in prayer – for better
is your prayer the closer
you come to Jesus and
Mary and the closer you get
the more you grow in that love
for Jesus and Mary.
            Let us pray

                    God bless you
                    M. Teresa M.C.


* LDM = "Laus Deo Mariaeque"

O Jesus,
In union with all the
Masses being offered
throughout the Catholic
world I offer thee my
heart. Make it meek
and humble like yours

Jesus in my heart I believe
in your faithful love for
me I love thee

O Jesus,
In union with all the
Masses being offered
throughout the Catholic
World I offer Thee my
heart. Make it meek
and humble like yours.


Jesus in my heart I believe
in your faithful love for
me I love Thee

Love others as
God loves you
Remember
Works of love
are
Works of Peace
God bless you
Mu Teresa mc
Love begins at home

Love others as
God loves you
        Remember
Works of love
        are
Works of Peace

        God bless you
        M. Teresa M.C.

Love begins at home

*Mother's prayers*

JESUS HAS DRAWN US TO BE
SOULS OF PRAYER

- With Jesus, for Jesus, to Jesus.
- Jesus, come into my heart. Pray in me and with me that I may learn from You how to pray.
- Jesus present in my heart, I adore You, I love You.
- Jesus in my heart, I believe in Your tender love for me. I love You.
- Jesus in my heart, I believe in Your faithful love for me. I love You.
- Jesus, I am grateful to You for all You have given me. I also offer You everything.
- I belong to You, Jesus.
- Because I belong to You, I want to give everything in me to You. Use me to the full. Don't mind my feelings so long as I remain completely Yours.
- Lord, don't allow my feelings to spoil the beautiful handiwork You have begun in my soul.
- Cut me into pieces. Every piece will be Yours.

- Humility of the Heart of Jesus, fill my heart.
- Purity of the Heart of Jesus, purify my heart.
- Charity of the Heart of Jesus, fill my heart.
- Jesus, I am here, love me!
- Since I cannot burn inside for love of You, I offer You the heat that I feel outside.
- Let me touch what You want me to touch. Let me see what You want me to see.
- Jesus, take away everything that is not You. I want my heart to be like Mary's heart.
- I will be all for Jesus through Mary.
- Jesus, for love of You.
- In the name of Jesus and for the love of Jesus and because Jesus has said it "that if anything we ask You in His name will be granted" grant me the grace to love You only, the grace of making my heart like the Heart of Jesus, meek and humble.
- In union with all the Masses being offered throughout the Catholic world, I offer You my heart, make it meek and humble like Yours.

- Jesus, silent in my heart, I adore Thee.
- Jesus, silent in my heart, I love Thee.
- Jesus in my mouth, let me not say that ugly word.
- Silence of the Heart of Jesus, speak to me, strengthen me.

- Heart of Jesus, make my heart pure through thoughtfulness, so that I can see You in my Sisters and the poor I serve.
- Heart of Jesus, burning with love for me and my Sister, inflame our hearts with love for each other.
- Jesus, go into the heart of my Sister.
- Jesus in her heart, I believe in Your faithful love for her. I love You for her. I offer all the Masses being offered just now for her.
- Please, let my Sisters grow in holiness.
- Jesus, make them only all for You.
- Soul of Christ, sanctify her, forgive her. She does not know what she says or does.
- Jesus in my Sister and in my heart, I believe in Your tender love for her and for me. She and I love You. Keep us in Your Heart.

- Jesus, Son of the living God, living in my heart, have mercy on me, a sinner.
- Thank you, Jesus, for taking away my sins.
- Make my heart clean.
- By Your most Precious Blood, wash me and purify me.
- Let me share with You Your pain. I want to be the Spouse of Jesus Crucified.
- Let me share Your loneliness, Your being unloved, uncared for.
- In union with all the Masses being offered throughout the world, I offer You this.
- Eternal Father, I offer Thee the Precious Blood of Jesus; and in union with the Blood of Jesus, I offer Thee my heart for the greater glory of Your Name and to satiate Your thirst for souls.

- Soul of Christ, sanctify them
  Body of Christ, save them
  Passion of Christ, strengthen them
  Within Thy Wounds, hide them
  Never let them be separated from Thee.
- Precious Blood of Jesus, save souls.
- In union with all the Masses being offered throughout the world, I offer Thee Jesus, for those in danger of dying without contrition.
- Eternal Father, I offer Thee Jesus, Thy Beloved Son and with Him I offer Thee my heart – in Him, with Him, through Him – to the greater glory of Your Name and so to satiate the thirst of Jesus for love of souls.

- Jesus, I come with a pure heart. Nothing and nobody can separate me from the love of You.
- I can love all, but the only one I will love in particular is You, only.
- Thank You, God! I want to be poor. I want to obey.
- Jesus in my heart, increase my faith, strengthen my faith. Let me live this faith through living humble obedience.
- I will give You whole-hearted free service in whatever form You come to me.
- Eternal Father, I offer Thee Jesus, Thy Beloved Son and I offer Thee myself with Him for the greater glory of Your Name and the good of souls.
- Dear God, give me the grace of perseverance.

MOTHER'S MEDITATION
(in the hospital, 19 June 1983)


WHO DO YOU SAY I AM?
[Matthew 16: 15]


You are God.
You are God from God.
You are Begotten, not made.
You are One in Substance with the Father.
You are the Son of the Living God.
You are the Second Person of the Blessed Trinity.
You are One with the Father.
You are in the Father from the beginning: All things were
made by You and the Father.
You are the Beloved Son in Whom the Father is well pleased.
You are the Son of Mary, conceived by the Holy Spirit in
the womb of Mary.
You were born in Bethlehem.
You were wrapped in swaddling clothes by Mary and put
in the manger full of straw.
You were kept warm by the breath of the donkey who
carried Your Mother with You in her womb.
You are the Son of Joseph, the Carpenter as known by the
people of Nazareth.

You are an ordinary man without much learning, as judged by the learned people of Israel.

## Who is Jesus to Me?

Jesus is the Word made Flesh.
Jesus is the Bread of Life.
Jesus is the Victim offered for our sins on the Cross.
Jesus is the Sacrifice offered at the Holy Mass for the sins of the world and mine.
Jesus is the Word – to be spoken.
Jesus is the Truth – to be told.
Jesus is the Way – to be walked.
Jesus is the Light – to be lit.
Jesus is the Life – to be lived.
Jesus is the Love – to be loved.
Jesus is the Joy – to be shared.
Jesus is the Sacrifice – to be offered.
Jesus is the Peace – to be given.
Jesus is the Bread of Life – to be eaten.
Jesus is the Hungry – to be fed.
Jesus is the Thirsty – to be satiated.
Jesus is the Naked – to be clothed.
Jesus is the Homeless – to be taken in.
Jesus is the Sick – to be healed.
Jesus is the Lonely – to be loved.

## IMMACULATE HEART OF MARY, CAUSE OF OUR JOY, BLESS YOUR OWN MISSIONARIES OF CHARITY

- Mary, Mother of Jesus, teach me to love Jesus as you love Him.

- Give me your Heart so beautiful, so pure, so immaculate, your Heart so full of love and humility that I may be able to receive Jesus in the Bread of Life and love Him as you love Him and serve Him in the distressing disguise of the poor.

- Mary, my Mother, be a Mother to me. Give me the strength, the conviction that I belong to Jesus and nothing will separate me.

- Mary, obtain for me purity of heart – a heart free from sin.

- Mary, Mother of Jesus, throw your mantle of purity over me and keep me pure for Jesus only.

- That I may love Jesus as you love Him – not only today – not only for one day, but every day.

- Mary, give me your Heart, so beautiful, so pure that I may know the greatness of Jesus.

- Humility of the Heart of Mary, fill my heart – teach me

as you taught Jesus to be meek and humble of heart and so glorify our Father.

- Mary, my Mother, give me your heart so pure, so immaculate, yet so humble that I may know Jesus as you know Him, that I may serve Jesus as you served Him. Obtain for me a pure and humble heart.

- Give me your Heart that I may love as you love.

- Silence of Mary, speak to me, teach me how – with you and like you – I can learn to keep all things in my heart as you did, not to answer back when accused or corrected – as you did.

- Give me your Heart so full of love and humility – help me to be pure like you, virgin like you.

- Mary, help us to make our hearts pure to be able to use obedience to become holy.

- Holiest Mother, we beg of you, lend us your heart so beautiful, so pure, so immaculate; your heart so full of love and humility.

- Mary, Mother of Jesus, make me only all for Jesus.

- Mary, Mother of Jesus, be a Mother to me now.

- Mary, Mother of Jesus, help me to be pure and humble like you, because I want to be holy and pleasing to the Blessed Trinity as you were and are.

A CONTEMPLATIVE IS A PERSON WHO LIVES TWENTY-FOUR HOURS WITH JESUS, FOR JESUS, IN JESUS; AND ALL SHE DOES IS TO JESUS THROUGH MARY

- Our silence demands of us constant self-denial and plunges us into the deep silence of God where aloneness with God becomes a reality.
- The Word of God is speechless today. In the Eucharist His silence is the highest and the truest praise of the Father.
- We need silence to be alone with God, to speak to Him, to listen to Him, to ponder His words deep in our hearts.
- In silence we are filled with the energy of God Himself that makes us do all things with joy.
- The fruit of silence is prayer, the fruit of prayer is faith, the fruit of faith is love and the fruit of love is service.
- To be only all for Jesus we need deep life of prayer. How do we learn to pray? – By praying.
- We have different litanies for the liturgical year. Each word is a cry of the soul. Let us try to understand its meaning, to taste the sweetness and enjoy the invoca-

tions calling Him. It is at these invocations that the Heart of Jesus opens Itself to our love and devotion.

- Silence is at the root of our union with God and with one another.

- Let us adore Jesus in the Eucharistic Silence.

- Souls of prayer are souls of great silence.

- We must endeavor to live alone with Jesus in the sanctuary of our inmost heart.

- In reality there is only one substantial prayer, Christ Himself. One voice which unites in itself all the voices raised in prayer.

- Perfect prayer does not consist in many words, but in the fervour of the desire which raises the heart to Jesus.

- Whatever we say in prayer, let it be with attention and great devotion so that our words may be written in letters of gold.

- How necessary it is for us to pray the work, to make the work our love for God in action.

- All our vocal prayers should be burning words coming forth from the furnace filled with love.

- Cling to the Rosary as the creeper clings to the tree, for without Our Lady we cannot stand.

- We must not only begin the day with prayer, but fill it with prayer and end it with prayer.

- Pray kneeling, pray with folded hands, with downcast

eyes and lifted hearts and your prayers will become like a pure sacrifice offered to God.

- Mental prayer is fostered by simplicity, forgetfulness of self; by mortification (of body and senses) and by frequent aspirations which feed our prayer.
- Contemplation of God is a gift of God to every Missionary of Charity.
- Contemplation is simply to realize God's constant presence and His tender love for us.
- We are called to be contemplatives in the heart of the world.
- Jesus in my heart, I believe in Your tender love for me; I love You.
- O what could my Jesus do more than give me His own flesh for my food?
- No, not even God could do more nor show a greater love for me.

Glory be to
                the Father — Prayer
And to
                the Son — Poverty
And to
    the Holy Spirit — Zeal for Souls

Amen — Mary.

# A chronological biography of Mother Teresa and the Missionaries of Charity

*August 26, 1910*  Born Agnes Gonxha Bojaxhiu, of Albanian parents at Skopje, Macedonia (Ex-Yugoslavia). Her parents Nikola and Dranafile Bojaxhiu had three children, the eldest a girl named Aga, followed by a boy named Lazar, and then Agnes who was the youngest.

*August 27, 1910*  Mother Teresa was baptized Agnes the day following her birth.

*November 16, 1916*  On this date she received the sacrament of Confirmation.

Mother Teresa attended the government school (Gimnaziya). While at school she became a member of the Sodality. Mother Teresa was still a young girl when she lost her father leaving her mother alone to raise the family. At that time Yugoslav Jesuits had accepted to work in the Calcutta Diocese the first group arriving in India on December 10, 1925. One of them was sent to Kurseong. From there he sent enthusiastic letters about the Bengal Mission Field. Those letters were read regularly to the Sodalists. Young Agnes was one of the sodalists who volunteered for the Bengal Mission. She was put in touch with the Loreto nuns in Ireland as they were working in Calcutta Archdiocese.

*September 25, 1928*  She joined the Irish Sisters of Loreto in Dublin, Rathfarnham.

*November 29, 1928*  She was sent to India to begin her novitiate in Darjeeling.

*January 6, 1929*  She arrived in Calcutta. (By ship) India – Bengal.

*May 23, 1929*  She entered into the novitiate in Darjeeling.

*May 24, 1931*  She took her first vows in Darjeeling and was sent to teach geography at St. Mary's High School in Calcutta. She took the name of Sister Teresa in honour of St. Theresa of the Child Jesus.

*May 24, 1937*  She took her final vows in Loreto, Darjeeling and returned to Calcutta. She became Mother Teresa and principal of the High School of St. Mary's in Calcutta. She was also in charge of the Daughters of St. Anne, the Indian Religious Order attached to the Loreto Sisters.

*September 9, 1946*  Mother Teresa departed by train for her annual retreat in Darjeeling from Calcutta.

*September 10, 1946*  "Inspiration Day" when on the train to Darjeeling Mother heard the call of God, to begin a new order that would satiate the thirst of Jesus for love and for souls by labouring at the salvation and sanctification of the Poorest of the Poor.

*January 1948*  Mother Teresa requested permission from her Superior General to live outside the cloister and to work in the Calcutta slums. She applied to Rome in February of 1948. From the beginning Mother depended only on Divine Providence sharing in the life of the poor.

*August 16, 1948*  Mother Teresa left Loreto, laid aside her Loreto habit and clothed herself in a white sari with a blue border and a cross on the shoulder. She went for three months to the American Medical Missionary Sisters for intensive nursing training.

*December 8, 1948*  She returned to Calcutta to stay temporarily with the Little Sisters of the Poor.

*December 21, 1948*  Mother Teresa went into the slums, visiting the poor and nursing the sick. She opened her first slum school in Motijheel, renting two rooms, one to be used for the school, the other was to be used as the first home for the sick and dying destitutes.

*1948* Mother Teresa becomes an Indian citizen.

*January 2, 1949* Mother wrote the first rule for the Society of the Missionaries of Charity.

*February 2, 1949* Mother moved into a flat in 14 Creek Lane. The flat was part of the home belonging to Michael Gomez.

*March 19, 1949* Subashini Das (Sister Agnes), a young Bengali girl, became the first to join Mother. That same year three more girls joined: Sr. Gertrude, Sr. Trinita and Sr. Dorothy.

*1949* The first dispensaries began to function. One being in St. Theresa's Church helped by Dr. Cecile Ghosh, another in Park Circus helped by Dr. Decruz. Later on in Kidderpor another dispensary was started.

*October 7, 1950* The new Congregation of the Missionaries of Charity was approved and instituted in Calcutta under the care of Archbishop Ferdinand Perier, S.J. with the Decree of Erection. There were twelve sisters at this date.

*April 11, 1951* The first group of sisters enter the novitiate.

*August 22, 1952* Mother opened the first Nirmal Hriday (Home for the sick and dying destitutes) in Calcutta. This home, Kalighat, had previously been a guesthouse for the Temple of Kali.

*January, 1953* Mother drafted the basis for the Link of Sick and suffering Co-Workers by proposing to Jacqueline de Decker the possibility of sick people to join in the work of the new order by offering their suffering in union with the work of a sister with whom they would be linked.

*1953* Mother opened the first Shishu Bhavan (Home for abandoned and malnourished children). From this home the works of food distribution, daily feeding, dispensary, and T.B. Clinic were also carried out. Adoption work also began with the local adoptions. This would eventually go beyond India.

*February, 1953* By this date the sisters had moved from Creek Lane to 54A Lower Circular Road. This new home became known as Mother House.

*April 12, 1953* Mother took her final vows as a Missionary of Charity and the first group took their first vows. The ceremony took place in the Cathedral and was presided over by His Excellency Rev. Perier, S.J.

*1955* By this year there were 48 sisters.

*September 1957* Mother opened her first mobile leprosy clinic. It was blessed by Archbishop Perier, S.J. By January 600 lepers were attending regularly. Dr. Sen devoted himself to helping Mother in this work.

*May 29, 1959* The first mission house outside Calcutta was founded at Ranchi in the Indian State of Bihar.

*October 7, 1961* The first General Chapter was held.

*April, 1962* Mother received the Padma Shri Award from the President of India. (Padma Shri meaning "Lotus at the feet of God".)

*September 1962* Mother received the Magsaysay Award for International Understanding given in honour of the late President of the Philippines.

*March 25, 1963* The Archbishop of Calcutta blessed the beginning of a new branch of the Missionaries of Charity, The Missionaries of Charity Brothers. (Active)

*1963* Pope Paul VI visited India and donated the Papal car to Mother.

*February 1, 1965* The Missionaries of Charity became a Society of Pontifical Right, with the Decree of Praise by Pope Paul VI.

*July 26, 1965* Mother and five sisters went to Venezuela to open the first foundation outside India. On the way to Venezuela they stopped in Rome where they had a private audience with Pope Paul VI.

*December 8, 1967* Mother took sisters to Ceylon to open a house in Colombo.

*August 22, 1968*  Mother went to Rome and opened a house in the slums of that city in Torfiscale.

*September 8, 1968*  Mother went to open a new foundation in Tanzania, the first foundation in Africa.

*March 29, 1969*  The International Association of Co-Workers of Mother Teresa was affiliated with the Order of the Missionaries of Charity and the Constitution of the Association was presented to His Holiness Pope Paul VI and received his blessing.

*September 30, 1969*  Mother went to open a home in Australia, Bourke, where the sisters would work among the aboriginal people.

*July 16, 1970*  Mother went to open a foundation in the Middle East, Amman, Jordan.

*December 8, 1970*  A novitiate was opened in England to train novices from Europe and the Americas. This novitiate would eventually be moved to Rome.

*January 6, 1971*  Mother was awarded the Pope John XXIII Peace Prize by Pope Paul VI.

*October 16, 1971*  Mother received the John F. Kennedy International Award.

*October 28, 1971*  Mother was awarded the Doctor of Humane Letters Degree in Washington.

*October 19, 1971*  Mother opened a house in the Bronx, New York. This was the first house in North America.

*November, 1972*  Mother was presented with the Jawaharlal Nehru Award for International Understanding by the Indian Government.

*April 1973*  Mother was presented with the Templeton Award for "Progress in Religion" by Prince Philip.

*August 22, 1973*  Mother opened a new foundation in Hodeida, Yemen.

*October 4, 1973* Mother opened a new foundation in Lima, Peru.

*November 23, 1973* A foundation was opened in Addis Ababa, Ethiopia.

*April 3, 1974* The Brothers opened a house in Phnom Penh, Cambodia.

*June 9, 1974* A new foundation was started in Palermo, Sicily.

*June 19, 1974* The "Mater et Magistra" Award was presented to Mother Teresa in America.

*July 18, 1974* A new house was opened in Papua, New Guinea.

*August 1975* Mother was awarded the FAO Medal in Rome.

*October 23, 1975* Mother was awarded the Albert Schweitzer Prize in the United States.

*1975* Twenty-fifth Anniversary Jubilee of the Missionaries of Charity celebrated in India with eighteen different religious denominations.

*1976* Mother received an Honorary Doctorate from Santiniketan, India.

*June 25, 1976* Mother founded the Missionaries of Charity, Contemplative Branch in New York. Sr. Nirmala was the superior of this new branch.

*1977* Mother received an Honorary Doctorate of Divinity from Cambridge University.

*1977* Mother received the Balzan International Prize in Rome.

*March 19, 1979* The Missionaries of Charity, Contemplative Brothers were founded in Rome.

*December 10, 1979* Mother Teresa was awarded the Nobel Peace Prize.

*March 22, 1980* Mother was awarded the Bharat Ratna (Pearl of India) Award; India's highest honour.

*June 10, 1982* Mother was awarded an Honorary Doctorate from Harvard University.

*May 24, 1983* Mother suffered her first heart attack. She was in Rome at the time.

*October 31, 1984* The Missionaries of Charity Fathers were founded.

*December 8, 1988* Mother went into the Soviet Union opening a house in Moscow. At this time Mother promised to open 15 houses in the Soviet Union, one for each of the Mysteries of the Holy Rosary.

*August 21, 1989* Mother suffered a second heart attack.

*May 1990* Mother visited Albania, returning to her homeland after 62 years.

*March 2, 1991* Mother opened the first foundation in Albania.

*June 6, 1991* Mother opened a house in Baghdad.

*December 24, 1991* While visiting the sisters and fathers in Tijuana, Mexico, Mother suffered another heart attack. Surgical intervention was done in San Diego, CA.

*August 1993* Mother suffered another heart attack in Delhi and was brought back to Calcutta for surgery.

*November 1993* Mother visited Shanghai, China.

*March 29, 1994* Mother went to Vietnam to open a foundation.

*August 20, 1996* Once more Mother suffered a severe cardiac attack that brought the whole world to its knees in prayer for her recovery.

*December 1996* Mother suffered yet another heart attack but was back in Mother House for Christmas.

*January 1997* Sisters from throughout the world gathered in Mother House (Calcutta) for a General Chapter.

*March 13, 1997* Sr. Nirmala M.C. was elected as the new Superior General of the Missionaries of Charity. She received a blessing from Mother.

*April 9, 1997* Sr. Agnes M.C., the first sister to have joined Mother when she began the order, died in Calcutta.

*May 1997*  Mother travelled with Sister Nirmala to Rome where she presented her new Superior General to the Holy Father John Paul II.

*June 1997*  Mother was presented with the Congressional Gold Medal in the United States.

*September 5, 1997*  At 8:57 p.m. in Mother House, the First Friday in September, Jesus took our Mother home.

*September 13, 1997*  Mother's body laid in state for the week following her death in St. Thomas Church. Thousands upon thousands of mourners passed by to pay their last respects. They came from all over the world and from all walks of life, both the rich and the poor. On the 13th of September Mother was given a State Funeral and was then laid to rest in Mother House itself.

*1998*  Active Sisters and Contemplative Sisters: nearly 4000 sisters in 124 countries (about 579 houses). Active Brothers and Contemplative Brothers: about 400 brothers. Fathers: 15 priests; about 35 men in different stages of formation.